My Little Golden
TRAINS

By Dennis R. Shealy
Illustrated by Paul Boston

The editors would like to thank Bob Lettenberger,
director of education at the National Railroad Museum,
for his assistance in the preparation of this book.

A GOLDEN BOOK • NEW YORK

Text copyright © 2021 by Penguin Random House LLC
Cover art and interior illustrations copyright © 2021 by Paul Boston
All rights reserved. Published in the United States by Golden Books, an imprint of
Random House Children's Books, a division of Penguin Random House LLC, 1745 Broadway,
New York, NY 10019. Golden Books, A Golden Book, A Little Golden Book, the G colophon,
and the distinctive gold spine are registered trademarks of Penguin Random House LLC.
rhcbooks.com
Educators and librarians, for a variety of teaching tools, visit us at RHTeachersLibrarians.com
Library of Congress Control Number: 2020930121
ISBN 978-0-593-17466-1 (trade) — ISBN 978-0-593-17467-8 (ebook)
Printed in the United States of America
10 9 8 7 6 5 4 3

Steel wheels *clickity-clack-clack* along the tracks. The train is pulling into the station! Are you ready to ride?

All aboard!

The long line of cars being pulled behind a locomotive engine is called a **train**. Trains that carry people are called **passenger trains**. Sometimes people ride trains short distances, to their jobs or to get to a nearby city. Other times people ride trains to visit places far away.

You can also ride a train just for fun!

Trains that carry coal, oil, food, and other products are called **freight trains**. These trains easily move goods hundreds—even thousands—of miles so that food gets to grocery stores, cars get to auto dealers, and toys get to toy stores.

These trains can be up to a mile long and are pulled by powerful engines. But the big engines haven't always existed. . . .

A long time ago, if people wanted to get somewhere, they had to walk, ride a horse, or take a boat. Horses and other animals pulled carts and carriages to move people and products from place to place. It was hard work!

After **steam engines** were developed, people used them to power machines in factories and mines. Inventors began to experiment with steam engines on wheels and tracks that could go across land. By the early 1800s, the first railways dedicated to using steam engines began operating in the United States.

Soon train tracks were all over the country. **Bridges** allowed the tracks to continue over canyons and rivers, and **tunnels** were dug through mountains. The Transcontinental Railroad was completed in the United States on May 10, 1869. It connected the West Coast with the East Coast.

Amazing feats of railroad engineering continue today. The Gotthard Tunnel in Switzerland, which is the longest and deepest tunnel in the world, allows trains to travel under the Alps.

The Danyang-Kunshan Grand Bridge in China is 102 miles long—the longest bridge in the world! It is part of a high-speed railway that connects Beijing and Shanghai, the country's largest cities.

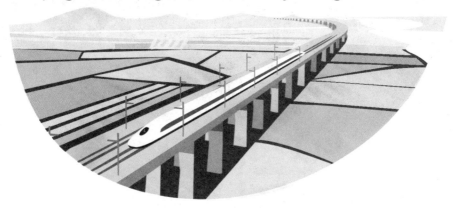

Early locomotives used wood or coal to
generate heat that boiled water to make steam.
The steam pressure turned the big wheels.

But all that wood and coal could produce a lot of smoke. And if the boilers weren't tended just right, steam engines could explode!

Big freight trains that travel long distances are now pulled by **diesel engines**, which are powered by fuel instead of coal or wood.

Many different types of cars can make up a freight train. For instance, coal and gravel are transported in open-top cars.

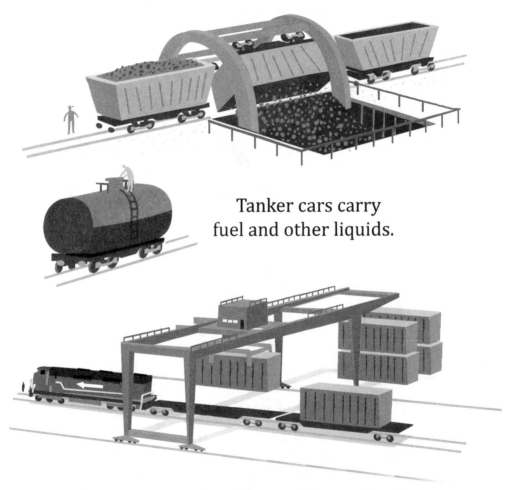

Tanker cars carry fuel and other liquids.

Refrigerator cars haul items that need to be kept cold. Just about everything else is moved with boxcars and flatbeds.

In some places, people ride trains to and from work every day. These are called **commuter trains**.

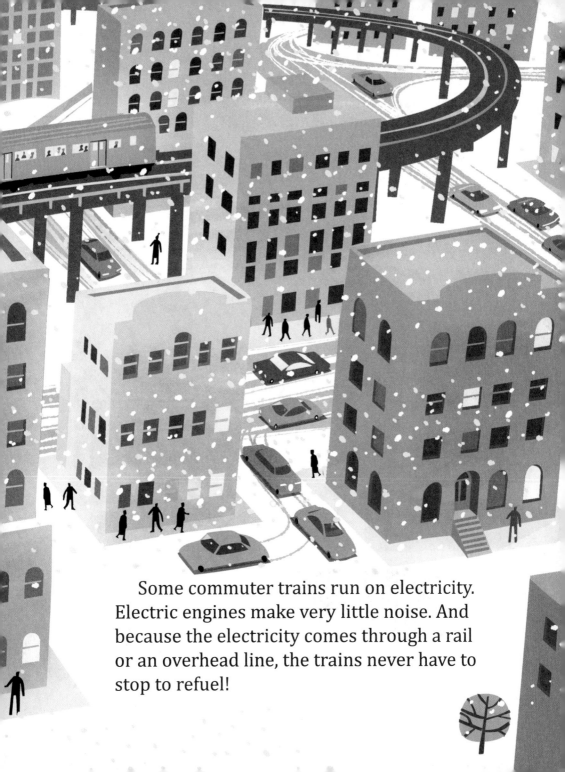

Some commuter trains run on electricity. Electric engines make very little noise. And because the electricity comes through a rail or an overhead line, the trains never have to stop to refuel!

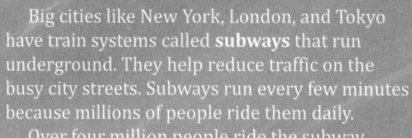

Big cities like New York, London, and Tokyo have train systems called **subways** that run underground. They help reduce traffic on the busy city streets. Subways run every few minutes because millions of people ride them daily.

Over four million people ride the subway in New York City every day!

Some countries in Asia and Europe have super-fast **bullet trains**. Commuters can ride them short distances, but the trains also allow riders to go long distances in a short time. Some bullet trains use wheels, while others use magnets to levitate and float above the tracks!

The Shanghai Maglev in China is the fastest bullet train in the world. Its top speed is 267 miles per hour!

Long-distance passenger trains have **dining cars**, where riders can have a bite to eat or something to drink while the countryside whizzes by.

Some of these trains also have **sleeper cars**. Riders can have a private room with a bed so they can sleep while the train rolls through the night.

Trains keep moving day and night, carrying people and freight wherever they need to go. So whenever you hear a train coming down the tracks, take a moment to imagine where it has been—

and where it is going!